PORTRAIT OF
NORWICH

ALAN CHILDS

HALSGROVE

First published in Great Britain in 2005

British Library Cataloguing-in-Publication Data
A CIP record for this title is available from the British Library

ISBN 1 84114 260 3

HALSGROVE

Halsgrove House
Lower Moor Way
Tiverton, Devon EX16 6SS
Tel: 01884 243242
Fax: 01884 243325
email: sales@halsgrove.com
website: www.halsgrove.com

Printed by D'Auria Industrie Grafiche Spa, Italy

To Reg and Ros with love

Introduction

Norwich is a city to be proud of: a city steeped in history, yet facing squarely the challenges of the twenty-first century. It has a castle started in the year following the Norman Conquest, and a cathedral begun within three decades after. But not far away from either of these, the city has a state-of-the-art Millennium library set in a building justly called 'the Forum'. This is a place of intermixing and happenings, or a place to sit and watch the world go by. There are major new developments under the shadow of the castle, and also along the riverside, and most recently in the area of Chapelfields. Throughout Norwich there is this juxtaposition of the old and the new. It is a city that rewards the traveller on foot, because down each of its narrow alleyways a new surprise is in store. In the same house in one modest courtyard for example, both Elizabeth Fry and Harriet Martineau were born. And Norwich started early: it was on a gravel terrace beside the river that the Saxon town *Norowic* was probably begun. When William decided to invade, Norwich was already one of the leading towns of the Saxon world, with its own mint. Moreover, throughout the medieval and Tudor periods, Norwich was considered second only in importance to London and had been a city from the time of Richard 1.

Norwich is a city of open spaces, the latter called 'plains' locally, but also of courtyards and alleyways. How many residents of Norwich can now pin-point these wonderful-sounding places: 'Labour in Vain Yard' or 'Vinegar Lane'; 'Butter Hills' or 'One Post Alley'; 'Gaffers Court' or 'Paradise Place'? It was claimed, in the late 1930s, that Norwich had a church for every Sunday and a pub for every day of the year. What is sometimes forgotten about this well-worn adage is that firstly, the 1930s total of pubs would probably have been exceeded a few decades earlier, and secondly that we are not talking comparatively 'ordinary' churches. There were probably sixty plus churches with origins in the medieval period – more than any other city in the country. Some 32 are still accounted for, although it must be said that with high maintenance costs and falling congregations, many have found other uses; one for example is now a popular puppet theatre. The names of these churches still trip off the tongue with a medieval mellifluence: St Giles on the Hill, St Peter Parmentergate, St Michael at Plea, St John Maddermarket, St Martin at Oak.

As for the pubs, there are so many, and so varied a list, that it is almost impossible to start. The 'Adam and Eve' claims to be the oldest, as befits its name, and each pub has a history, albeit a dark one, as in the case of the 'Murderers' café-bar in Timberhill. Some have had, over the centuries, an association with craft guilds and perhaps adopted their names accordingly – The Gardeners', the Bakers', the Butchers' or the Coachmakers' Arms. The names if not the associations are still there and the coats of arms sometimes appear on the pub signs. Some adapt to modern opportunities such as the 'Rouen', whose name was changed to reflect the twinning with that city or the 'Sir Garnet Wolseley', near the market, in commemorating a national hero in Victorian times. Others like 'The Dolphin', a former bishop's palace no less, and the 'Jack of Newbury', are pubs no more, yet the particular style of the woodwork or the ornamentation still shout out the building's former use. It is a fascinating study in its own right.

It goes almost without saying, that Norwich has other more obvious gems of architecture, as for example the Octagon Chapel in Colegate, the Great Hospital in Bishopgate (almost a well-kept secret), Norwich's Roman Catholic Cathedral of St John, a fine Victorian building, and of course the great Norman cathedral church of the Holy Trinity. This was Bishop de Losinga's masterpiece of inspired building, and it has the rare remains of a Saxon 'cathedra', or Bishop's seat, at the east end – albeit imported from North Elmham. The cathedral is second only to Salisbury in height, and has an astonishing collection of more than 1000 roof bosses telling their unique story in stone. There are also well-preserved cloisters and a beautiful cathedral Close. Together with the castle keep, the cathedral still dominates the city. It is always there, nudging into every view.

Norwich also has in its 'Assembly House' an elegant Georgian meeting place and concert venue, snatched back to life from an almost fatal fire in 1995 and painstakingly restored by craftsmen who, as at Windsor Castle, had to re-learn old skills in the process. Norwich has a medieval guildhall, the seat of Government until the twentieth century, and a much-visited street of cobblestones and jettied houses, called Elm Hill. Amazingly, both the Guildhall and Elm Hill were almost lost to urban 'clearance' a few decades ago, when conservation and redevelopment were viewed with very different eyes from today's. Much credit must be given to the determined and consistent work of the 'Norwich Society' in its watching brief and influential interventions. Every city needs the like!

Meandering through the city is the River Wensum, which has witnessed all the exciting, and turbulent happenings of the centuries: the bloody riots and the devastating plagues – and the almost inevitable fires. The river has offered part pleasure and part serious participation in the life of the city, from its early supporting-role in Norwich's defensive ring of walls. Today modern housing-developments line the waterside in the way industrial developments did previously. In the latter context, it is a city that has adapted to change: from the opportunities that were presented by the 'Strangers' of the sixteenth century, bringing new methods of cloth-making from the Low Countries, to the development of a flourishing boot and shoe industry in the nineteenth and twentieth centuries.

And there is a group of major industrial and business names that have affected the city's life over the last two hundred years or so: names such as Colman and Copeman; Caley and Jarrold; Southall, Norvic and Sexton; Boulton & Paul, Mann Egerton and Laurence Scott; Panks, Bonds and Barnards; and of course the important breweries: Bullard's and Morgan's, Young's and Steward & Patteson's. Such a range of innovative industries, from cars to printing and boots; from mustard to chocolate; from electro-motors to aeroplanes. And in the Quaker families, for example the Gurneys, the origins of modern banking were forged in this city, as the development of insurance was likewise fostered by the Norwich Union. At the heart of Norwich of course is the great market, one of the biggest in the country and open six days a week. Its history is continuous from Norman times, and it is an area few visitors neglect. In Norwich's small specialist shops also, some businesses have survived the decades, as for example 'Winsor Bishop' (Winsor was a Christian name), goldsmiths and silversmiths, still trading behind its impressive 1830s shop-front; or the family firm of 'Dipple and Son', jewellers, under its venerable swan clock. There are many others.

In more recent years the impact of the prestigious university has been felt, with the complementary developments of the Research Park (with for example the John Innes Centre), the Sainsbury Centre and the University Hospital.

To encapsulate the spirit of Norwich within a few pages is an impossible task and this collection is a personal choice, offering merely a fleeting glance; the city would reward a lifetime's study and some have made it such. Perhaps Nikolaus Pevsner was indeed right when he declared 'Norwich has everything'!

Alan Childs, June 2005

Acknowledgements

Acknowledgements and sincere thanks to all the following individuals and bodies:

Mr A. Anderson; Mr R. Baldwin; Dr A. Bell; Mrs A. Brennan (Maddermarket); Castle Mall Management; Mrs S. Childs; Charles Church (former Norfolk and Norfolk Hospital development); Mr P. Connor; Mrs N. Cox; Dean and Chapter, Norwich Cathedral; Dipple and Son; The Forum Trust Ltd; Mr and Mrs P. Gaskin; Mr L. Goreham; Ms L. Gray (Maddermarket); Mrs L. Haywood; Mr K. Holman; Mr and Mrs B. Houghton (and The Crescent, Norwich Ltd); B.W. Irving (Dentists); Jarrold and Sons Ltd; Mr and Mrs J. Lane; Mr D. MacKenzie; Maids Head Hotel; Millennium Library (Norfolk Heritage Centre); Norwich City Council; Norwich Union (Aviva plc); Plantation Garden Preservation Trust; Mr A. Pond; St John's Catholic Cathedral; Mr P. Stimpson (Maddermarket); Tower House, Bracondale; University of East Anglia; Wensum Lodge; Winsor Bishop.

Priest in charge and churchwardens of the churches of St Giles, St John Timberhill, St Julian, St Peter Mancroft.

Victorian pillar boxes are comparatively rare, but those that survive have an elegance of design. The one shown here, situated opposite City Hall, was the design of the architect and surveyor J. W. Penfold, who had been commissioned by the Postmaster General to come up with a new idea.

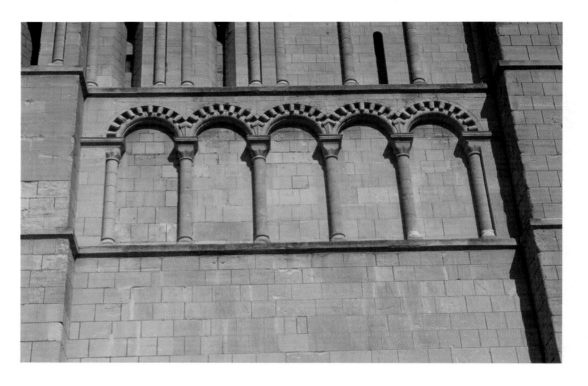

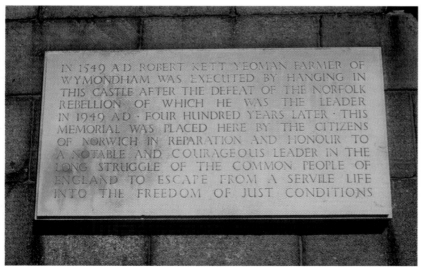

IN 1549 A.D. ROBERT KETT YEOMAN FARMER OF
WYMONDHAM WAS EXECUTED BY HANGING IN
THIS CASTLE AFTER THE DEFEAT OF THE NORFOLK
REBELLION OF WHICH HE WAS THE LEADER
IN 1549 A.D · FOUR HUNDRED YEARS LATER · THIS
MEMORIAL WAS PLACED HERE BY THE CITIZENS
OF NORWICH IN REPARATION AND HONOUR TO
A NOTABLE AND COURAGEOUS LEADER IN THE
LONG STRUGGLE OF THE COMMON PEOPLE OF
ENGLAND TO ESCAPE FROM A SERVILE LIFE
INTO THE FREEDOM OF JUST CONDITIONS

The Castle still dominates the city's skyline, as it has done for over 900 years. It was built, first of wood, on an artificial mound, and its lines of fortifications spread far out from the central keep. For much of its life it was a gaol, but it was opened as a museum in 1894. In the 1830s an architect, Anthony Salvin, 'restored' the castle's exterior (not without opposition), refacing the keep in Bath stone. The 'arcading' was not changed however, and the inside of the keep remains as 'raw' Norman stonework. Outside the main entrance is the sombre memorial to Norfolk's famous rebel, Robert Kett of Wymondham, leader of Kett's Rebellion (1549).

Norwich market has been at the hub of the city since the Normans moved it here and watched over it from their great castle. In medieval times there were rows of similar traders – the butchers' row, or the mercers' row. It is one of the largest markets in England. Things are still changing in the market, as they have over the centuries, but change to established ways is hard to take.

There is always a beady eye on the best strawberries.

Displaying fruit and vegetables to perfection is a great art. The angles of the fruit are just right and the labels complement the displays – market-stall calligraphy at its best.

Nothing can beat a flower stall for sheer rainbow brilliance; even the butterflies are larger than life!

Market-stall artwork always lends atmosphere.

Natasha Cox, ready for a new day on the market.

A study in expression at the bottom of the market. Alexander Pond's family (he's the one with the flower) has been here for 200 years. Alexander will sell flowers for every occasion.

The City Hall provides a fine backdrop to the market on a sunny day, with a spot of 'mardling' going on in the foreground. 'Foreigners' consult the 'Norfolk Dictionary'!

'Waiting for the off': last-minute preparations
for the Lord Mayor's Processsion

A fiery float whose participants are happy to pose!

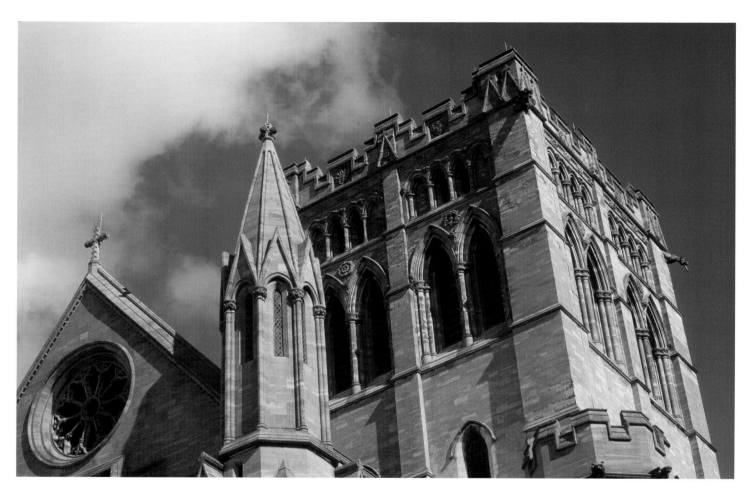

The Roman Catholic Cathedral (since 1976) of St John the Baptist at St Giles Gate, is an impressive Victorian building in a commanding position. It was begun in 1884 as a commission by the 15th Duke of Norfolk, and was completed in 1910. The design was by George Gilbert Scott Jun., and was continued by his brother John Oldrid Scott.. It contains both very fine nineteenth century stained glass, and stone carving.

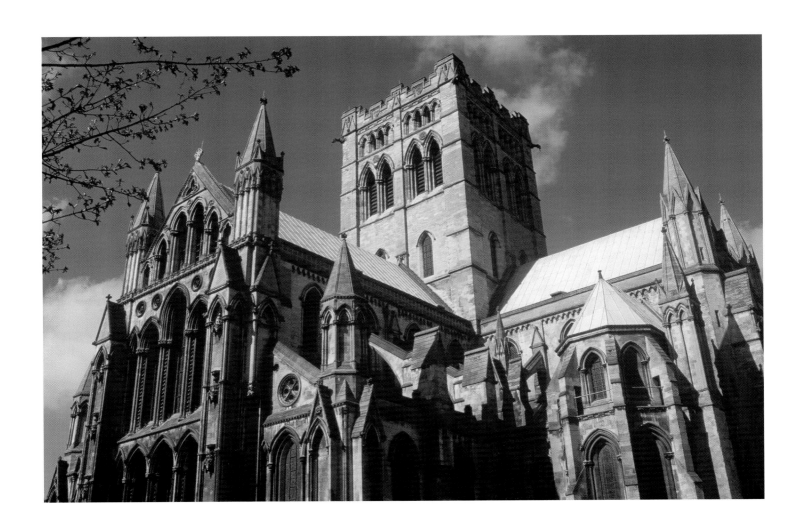

Chapelfield Gardens are at the centre of the small district of Chapelfield, once belonging to the College of St Mary (the Chapel of Our Lady in the Fields). The college began as a charitable 'hospital' in Norman times and after the Reformation fell into private hands, including the Hobarts. The open field was later granted to the city and was used for archery and military musters – even as a plague cemetery. When in 1877 Chapelfields was laid out as a public park, it contained for a time an impressive award-winning pagoda, designed by Thomas Jekyll. Today it has something for all ages to enjoy.

The popular band-stand in Chapelfield Gardens.

Will Kempe danced his way into the history books in February to March 1600, when he decided to leave his career as a comic actor, and to 'morris dance' from London to Norwich. The 'Nine Days' Wonder' was his dance between these cities – with a few breathing spaces in between of course. When the dancer arrived in Norwich, vast crowds welcomed him, and the Lord Mayor feasted him. Today he is commemorated in Chapelfield Gardens.

Will Kempe is reputed to have leaped over a wall near the church of St John Maddermarket (see p.75).

Always a background of flowers to the multitude of activities in the gardens, whatever the season.

A spot to sit and relax, with wild flowers still allowed their place.

Children's (and granddads') play area.

What is the collective name for a group of clocks? A 'striking' of clocks perhaps? Norwich has fine clocks in abundance:

The Cathedral clock is over the entrance to the south transept.

St. Michael at Plea: the church was associated with the Archdeacon's court, hence the name.

The Royal Arcade clock was designed by the architect George Skipper.

St Clement's clock is a modern-designed war memorial.

The Nat. West Bank could easily be confused for a Wren church.

St. Giles on the Hill has a very attractive clock-face.

Dipple and Son Jewellers, in Swan Lane, may stand on the site of the former Swan Inn. The Swan, made of beaten copper, was commissioned by the Dipple family.

The woodwork of this old door dates to the seventeenth-century house of Thomas Anguish (1538-1617), Mayor in 1616, which stood on this site. He endowed a 'hospital' in Fishergate for poor children (the 'Bluecoat' schools).

Victorian 'mock Tudor' belies the age of the 'Maids Head' Hotel. It claims to be the oldest in the city, dating back to the thirteenth century (although not with this name). Its period splendour is a must for visitors to the city. The Hotel is said to be on the site of the original Bishop's Palace. It saw bloodshed in front of its doors in Kett's Rebellion, and was the departure point for the first regular stage coach to London in 1762, the so-called 'Norwich Machine'.

There are fine railings at the perimeter of the station.

Norwich 'Thorpe' Station is the 'flagship' station for Norfolk. It was built in 1886 as the terminus of the Great Eastern Railway. The station, designed by John Wilson, has a fine façade, described as being in the 'French Chateau style'. The name 'Thorpe' derived from the area of the city in which it is situated, and distinguished it from Norwich's former Victoria and City stations. The station made a brief appearance in the locally shot film The Go Between (1970).

The statue of Lord Nelson (1758-1805), by Thomas Milnes, stands near to the Cathedral's west end. It is appropriately placed, as for a time the young Nelson attended the then 'King Edward VI Grammar School' based in the Close (as well as the ancient Paston Grammar School, in North Walsham). Nelson was born in the village of Burnham Thorpe near the coast, where his father Edmund was rector. Throughout his life he maintained a deep affection for his home county and his title 'Baron Nelson of the Nile and Burnham Thorpe', reflected this.

Thomas Browne (1605-82) was a remarkable man by the standards of any century. He was a research physician, a scientist, a philosopher and a writer. To most Norwich people he would have been simply a local doctor. It was a great honour to him and to the city that he was knighted here by Charles II, in 1671. His statue, not far from the church of St Peter Mancroft, where he is buried, overlooks his former Haymarket home. His most famous work is probably 'Religio Medici'.

Edith Cavell (1865-1915) is one of Norfolk's true heroines. She was born at Swardeston in Norfolk, and during the First World War served in Belgium as a nurse. She became involved in assisting allied servicemen to escape capture by crossing into Holland. She was arrested by the Germans in 1915, put on trial and shot. Her statue is near the Erpingham Gate to the cathedral, and her grave is close to the eastern end of the Cathedral, in the old monks' cemetery called 'Life's Green'.

The Assembly House is a jewel among Norwich's public buildings. It was built in 1734 by Thomas Ivory between two earlier wings, and was a town house for the Hobarts of Blickling Hall. After the last war, a wealthy shoe magnate, H.J.Sexton, generously restored it and gave it to the city. In 1995 it suffered a terrible fire, but has been brought to life following the most painstaking recreation of its former period details.

It is amazing to consider that in 1908 only the casting vote of the then mayor saved Norwich's ancient Guildhall from destruction. The building was the seat of Norwich's government for 500 years, only finishing in 1938 when the new City Hall was built.

Left: Norwich's coast of arms incorporated in the entrance arch to the Guildhall.

Right: 'Knapped' and squared flints in the wall of the Guildhall.

Fine chequer-work on the face of the Guildhall, perhaps a reference to the 'chequer table' on which taxes were calculated.

The clock was added in the nineteenth century.

The ubiquitous pigeons find a home in the nooks and crannies of the building.

The City Hall design has never been universally loved by locals, although over the years it has grown into its city centre role, overlooking the market. Certainly its sheer size dominates the area. It was designed by C.H. James and S.R. Pierce, following a design competition. King George VI opened the building in 1938. Look out for the fine bronze doors, by James Woodford, which contain panels showing the city's industries and major historical events.

Two bronze 'heraldic' lions, designed by Alfred Hardiman, guard the main doorway to the City Hall. One of these was exhibited at the British Empire exhibition of 1936 where it was seen by the architect of the new building. He commissioned a second lion.

OUR GLORIOUS DEAD

THEIR NAME LIVETH FOR EVERMORE

November's 'poppy-time' at the City of Norwich's war memorial in front of the City Hall. The memorial, designed by Sir Edwin Lutyens, was originally at the foot of the Guildhall. It was moved to its present site with the completion of the City Hall. Lutyens uses the 'cenotaph' – the empty tomb.

St Peter Mancroft (the name refers to the great field, the 'magna crofta' below the castle) has a Norman pedigree, but the present building dates from 1430-55. During the Civil War's fighting, a gunpowder explosion shattered a great deal of its medieval stained glass. The scale of this magnificent church is 'cathedral-like'.

'The Forum' is a most appropriate name for the mix of people and occasions that underpins the daily life of the building: a major interactive library, a TV and radio station, a Tourist Information Centre and cafes and sitting areas. In a different context the Roman forum must have worked in the same way. As a building there is a fascinating interplay of light and glass, combined with frag-mented reflections of buildings nearby. This innovative building, designed by Sir Michael Hopkins, was mainly completed in 2001 and is on the site of the old Central Library, lost to fire in 1994.

Thank goodness Norwich still has a few red telephone boxes. They are part of our history, even if they are time-consuming to paint! This one stands close to St Peter Mancroft whose railings here give a delightful pattern of shadows.

'Oh to be in England ...' as when near St Peter Mancroft, blossom and dappled shadows add a touch of magic to a well-loved pathway.

The Plantation Garden is a hidden gem, a secret garden in the heart of the city, under the shadow of St John's Roman Catholic Cathedral. It was created over a period of forty years (1856-1897) by Henry Trevor, a successful Norwich businessman, on the site of an abandoned chalk quarry. He borrowed ideas from Italian Renaissance gardens, and imported exotic plants. The materials that make up the walls are a fascinating and eclectic mix. By 1980 the garden was totally overgrown, but very fortunately the Plantation Garden Preservation Trust was formed and the miraculous restoration work was begun.

The Great Hospital, originally St Giles Hospital, was founded in 1249 by Walter de Suffield, Bishop of Norwich. It was a sanctuary for the sick, the needy and the aged, and in its beginning 13 poor people were allowed a daily meal – and a warm by the fire. Queen Anne of Bohemia visited in 1383 and the eagle ceiling in the hospital church of St Helen was created in her honour. Today in expanded accommodation, 125 or so residents are cared for in a tradition that has lasted seven-and-a-half centuries.

One of the most popular views of the city is from the top of Mousehold Heath. It has been much painted and photographed, as every season and time of day brings a different light and atmosphere to the panorama.

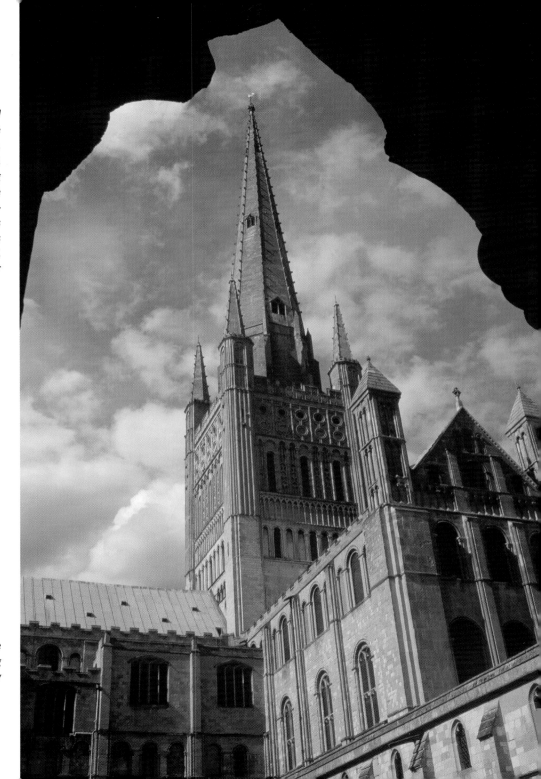

Norwich Cathedral, the church of the Holy and Undivided Trinity, was founded in 1096 by Herbert de Losinga and its Norman origins are still very evident. Most of the stone used was from Caen, in Normandy, with Norfolk flints as a core. Work on the building and the Benedictine monastery that was part of the plan, continued throughout Bishop de Losinga's lifetime, but it was not until 1278 that the cathedral was at last consecrated. Of the many fine features are its 1000 roof bosses, the remains of its Saxon 'cathedra', or bishop's throne, and the choir-stalls with their misericords.

The present spire replaced the former wooden spire which was destroyed by fire in 1463, after being struck by lightning. At 315 feet it is beaten only by Salisbury.

Details of the stonework of the beautiful central tower.

The cloisters where the monks might work, are the largest in any English cathedral. The roof bosses in the cloisters are of course more easily viewed.

The cathedral had five gates, including the 'water-gate', of which four survive as they originally were. This photograph shows the Erpingham Gate (c 1420) built by 'good old Sir Thomas Erpingham' of Shakespeare's 'Henry V'. He led the English archers at Agincourt and lived in Palace Plain.

St. George and the Dragon, in this modern replacement of original stonework, was by Mr Frank Beverley of Norwich.

The Ethelbert Gate (c1316) was built as a penance by the citizens for the Riots of 1272, in which the church of this name, just inside the precincts, was destroyed. It has been much restored over the centuries, but still has a great deal if interest, including the 'rose window' designs in flint and stone; this is called 'flushwork' as the two materials are 'flush' with each other.

Around the Cathedral is 'The Close', a microcosm of architectural history, and surely one of the most beautiful of any in England. There is evidence of the former monastic buildings, incorporated in later developments. The elegant No. 57 was built in 1862 and stands on the site of the former medieval 'plumbery', where the lead was fashioned for holding the stained glass.

52

Hook's Walk links the Lower Close to Bishopgate.

'Dutch gables', so often seen in Norfolk, reflect the area's connections with the Low Countries.

The house on the left is originally medieval, but has a 'Gothic' façade. On the right is the sacrist's house, also medieval in origin.

*No. 33 in the Lower Close, formerly called 'Brewery Green':
the houses in this part were built on the site of the old
monastic brewhouse and date from 1682.*

A feline resident of the Close taking the sun in Hook's Walk.

The west doorway of the cathedral, with its intricate stone carvings.

The 'Adam and Eve' (1247) claims to be the oldest pub in the city, probably with some justification. In its earliest days it was owned by the monks of The Great Hospital, who brewed here. The pub even has a ghost – that of Lord Sheffield, killed nearby in Kett's Rebellion. George Borrow, the writer patronized the pub, as did the infamous nineteenth century 'Stanfield Hall' murderer, James Rush.

Opposite: The 'Sir Garnet Wolseley' pub commands a superb position between the market and St Peter Mancroft, and is a fine building. Sir Garnet Wolseley (1833-1913) had a distinguished army career, including the Crimea and the Indian Mutiny. He is remembered as leader of the expedition that attempted to save General Gordon in 1884-5. By the year 1886 the pub had been renamed in his honour.

The 'Gardeners' Arms' in Timberhill was the original name for the adjoining 'Murderers Café Bar', but the latter rather macabre title came about from the real murder of a young girl. Old pubs in the city often reflected trade groups and craft guilds in their names.

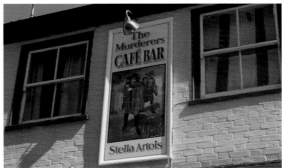

There are not many pubs that can claim a previous existence as a Bishop's Palace, but the former 'Dolphin Inn' in Heigham Street can certainly do so. Built in 1541 by Richard Browne, who held the office of sheriff, it became the home of Bishop Joseph Hall, who lived here 1643-59. It later became the 'Dolphin Inn'. This impressive flint building was badly damaged in the 1942 air-raids, and remained a ruin for many years until Steward and Patteson's Brewery restored it to its present condition.

The 'Woolpack Inn' in Golden Ball Street, with its large brass sign, was opened in 1938. A selection of newspapers of the day was sealed inside the woolpack sign, for future generations to find.

The former 'Norfolk and Norwich Hospital' in St Stephen's Road was rebuilt between 1879-83 by the local architect Edward Boardman and the London architect, Sit Thomas Wyatt. Parts of the old buildings are incorporated in a prestigious housing development.

The Rosary Cemetery, strange as it may seem, is a delight-fully atmospheric place to visit, set on its hillside site. It was the first private cemetery in the country, and was founded by a Presbyterian Minister, Revd Thomas Drummond. It was opened in 1821 and is probably the oldest non-denomina-tional cemetery in England. Many of the city's famous names are buried here, such as R.H. Mottram, John Jarrold and the artist James Stark.

The 'Royal Arcade' is a lasting legacy to the sheer imagination and flair of George Skipper (1856-1948). It was built in 1899 on the site of the Royal Hotel, which moved to Agricultural Hall Plain. The 'Art Nouveau' concept used glazed Doulton tiles, decorated with peacocks. The east end window has stylized trees in stained glass. Italian workmen were even brought over to lay the tesselated pavement.

66

The now famous University of East Anglia with its residential 'ziggurats', angular blocks and elevated walkways, achieved high aclaim when the University opened in the 1960s – but not of course universally! The design was by Denys Lasdun (additions by Sir Bernard Feilden) and the university was built on the site of the former Earlham Golf Course. A feature of the landscaping was a man-made 'broad' adjoining the River Yare.

Earlham Hall was the former home of the Gurney family and Elizabeth Fry grew up here. It now serves as the UEA's School of Law.

Castle Mall is a development of nearly 7 acres under the shadow of the Norman castle, and lying within the area of the southern 'outer bailey' of its original defences. An archaeological dig, in 1989, preceded the development and the Mall opened to the public in September 1993.

Elm Hill was originally a busy street, and with its cobblestones was typical of many others. Today it is a lone survivor, the street that every visitor to Norwich loves to explore. It has every reason for its fame, even if it was one councillor's vote in the 1920s that saved it from 'slum clearance'. The Norwich Society, as elsewhere in the city, played a large part in keeping this important street in being, with the 'Strangers' Club' an early success. Sadly the fine old elm tree at the top succumbed to disease some years ago.

'Jettied' buildings are evidence of timber framing that is sometimes concealed. Each storey protrudes a little further than the one below.

One of the fascinating courtyards off Elm Hill.

The root of the madder plant gave Norwich weavers their red dye; the Maddermarket Theatre and the Church of St John nearby, take their name from this ancient market. The theatre was founded by Nugent Monck in 1921 and has since been the home of the Norwich Players. Inside, the stage and galleries are based on a Shakespearian original, but with no outside elements to contend with! It is built on the site of an eighteenth century Roman Catholic chapel. The 'planning meeting', outside, comprises Averil Brennan (Chairman of the Theatre Trust), Linda Gray (set-designer) and Paul Stimpson (technical director).

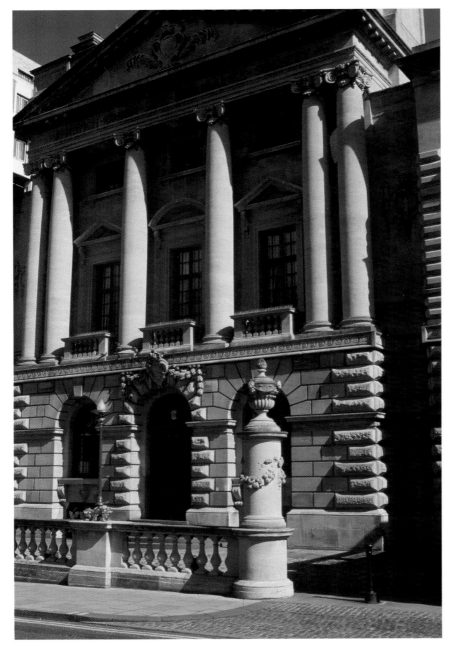

Surrey Street took its name from Surrey Court, the palace of the Earl of Surrey (eldest son of Henry VIII's Duke of Norfolk). The Norwich Union acquired the building in 1907 and on its site George Skipper built Surrey House, home of the Norwich Union.

An interesting lamp outside one of the Norwich Union buildings in Surrey Street.

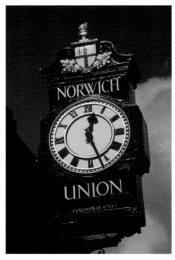

The Norwich Union's famous clock weighs 6 cwt and was put up in 1927.

The founder of the Norwich Union, Sir Samuel Bignold.

The clock-tower of Norwich Prison — surely the slowest moving clock in the city!

The 'Cow Tower' played a part in the city defences, its name possibly deriving from cattle sheltering in, or near it. It was rebuilt entirely of brick by the 'city' in 1399, it being previously under the control of the Prior, and then the Great Hospital. It was formerly called 'Dungeon Tower' and its original use was as a tollhouse from which the prior's servants collected river tolls.

Old and new: Norwich has many sections of its old city walk (begun 1294) still surviving.

While the Chapelfield development was taking place, the city's skyline was dominated by cranes.

'Cranescape' would seem to be a fitting title for this photograph!

St. Giles on the Hill has the highest tower (120 feet) of any of the city churches. The tower once served as a beacon, with a fire being lit in an iron basket. The church, with its gruesome gargoyles, dates from about 1420 and the cupola from 1737. It has a delightful churchyard with interesting architecture from the backs of houses in Willow Lane. Every May the front of the churchyard is swathed in wisteria.

Part of the old cemetery in Earlham Road has been designated a wildlife area. Here squirrels crack nuts on the gravestones, and the soft light of early autumn attracts an insect world. It is reminiscent of a country churchyard.

Sundial on St. Peter Mancroft.

Sundial on the 'Old Meeting House', Colegate.

The Old Meeting House in Colegate was built for the 'Independents'. They were early Congregationalists who had met locally from late Tudor times. Their chapels were 'independent' of one another, hence the name. In 1693 this splendid meeting house was built, with pilasters and capitals, and possibly the first sash windows in the city.

The Octagon Chapel, close to the Old Meeting House, in Colegate, was built in 1756 with bricks from Mousehold Heath. It was designed by Thomas Ivory as the 'New Meeting House', and became the centre for the City's Dissenters. John Wesley thought it 'perhaps the most elegant one (meeting house) in all Europe'. By the beginning of the nineteenth century the congregation had transferred their loyalties to Unitarianism.

The former Martineau Memorial Hall and Sunday School in Colegate: Harriet Martineau was a writer, and her brother James a Unitarian theologian. The family was of Huguenot origin. By chance, Harriet was born in the same house (in Gurney Court) where Elizabeth Fry (née Gurney) had previously been born.

89

Colegate is generally regarded as one of the richest streets, architecturally, in the whole of Norwich. It has the church of St Clement, associated with Archbishop Parker, and buildings from the medieval period through to the nineteenth century. At one time the Norvic Shoe factory dominated the centre of the street, when the Norwich shoe industry was exceptionally important. One of the most interesting houses here, of flint and timber, is the Bacon House, the home of Henry Bacon a rich worsted merchant, who was mayor in 1557 and 1566. It was built in 1548 to celebrate his year as Sheriff.

On the beams of the back area of the Augustine Steward House can be seen the original carpenter's marks – the Roman numerals that ensured timber buildings 'laid down' in the yards would fit together when, like a kit, they were assembled on site.

Augustine Steward's house is not one to view after a party, but the leaning windows are quite genuine! It was built in 1549 by a merchant, Augustine Stewart, who held Kett's rebels at bay. Through the archway are raised areas said to contain the remains of layer upon layer of the bones of plague victims who died in the Black Death of 1349 – one quarter of the city's population it is thought.

Norwich has a remarkably fine collection of doorways from the eighteenth and nineteenth centuries.

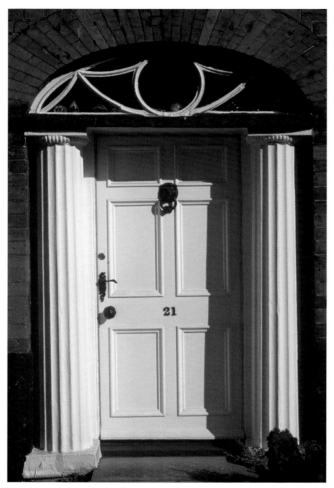

The doorway of No. 21 Sussex Street.

The doorway of No. 22 Sussex Street.

The doorway of Tower House, Bracondale; it is so named because of the tower at its rear. The house is still used as a base for circuit judges, when the Union Jack of course flies in front.

The doorway of No. 93 Pottergate.

St Julian's Church was where 'Mother Julian' of Norwich, a fourteenth century anchoress, wrote 'Revelations of Divine Love', considered to be the first book in English by a female writer. The church where St. Julian's cell is found was badly damaged in an air raid in 1942, but has been reconstructed.

Amongst the tableau of ancient buildings in King Street, one of the oldest streets in the city, is 'Dragon Hall'. It was built in about 1450 by Robert Toppes, a wealthy cloth merchant, as a merchant's hall, where he would display his goods. The building was lost to centuries of concealment, divided into smaller parts. Now with its timber-framed great hall and crown post roof with a 'dragon' in one of the spandrels, its 'screens passage' and vaulted undercroft, it is a 'must' for visitors to the city. The stone figures possibly represent 'harmony and strife'.

A pleasant range of old buildings in King Street.

Over the entrance to the former 'Ship' pub, in King Street, is this fine lintel. It was brought here from the redundant 'Princes Inn' in Princes Street.

The 'Old Music House' has a seventeenth-century front that conceals its ancient origins. It is probably the oldest domestic building in the city, dating to the early thirteenth century, and owned originally by Isaac Jurnet. Its musical connection was with the City 'Waits' – a group of singers who practised here.

This mural is perhaps little seen except by those attending courses at Wensum Lodge Study Centre, where it adorns one of the inward-facing walls. It was painted by Walter Kershaw, a north country artist, to commemorate Norwich Industry Year, 1986.

This mural 'relief' of St Stephen's Gate (or Nedeham Gate), one of the original 12 gates of the city, was designed by the Italian artist Moray-Smith. A second was completed of the Ber Street gate. The artist was also responsible for a series of reliefs inside the 'Woolpack Inn'.

Bracondale is an area of Norwich with a distinct character, and many fine period houses such as the 'Manor House'. The present gabled building dates from about 1617 and was probably built for Ann Kempe, the widow of a wealthy Norwich grocer. The term 'manor house' has no historical significance. In 1890 it was acquired by Jeremiah James Colman, the founder of the Mustard firm, but he did not live here. During the last war it was the H.Q. for the local A.T.S under Commander Wood, daughter of the conductor, Sir Henry.

*From Georgian through Regency to Victorian and the 1930s, Bracondale
has something to offer everyone in its architectural landscape.*

Even without its summer foliage, the ornate ironwork is a rare feature at Chapel Field House.

Chapelfield North has a pleasant mixture of buildings that have equal interest with winter or spring light on them. Park House is nearest the camera.

A pleasant nineteenth century terrace in Unthank Road with impressive bay windows. The name of the road has an 'Alice in Wonderland' feel, but is named after Colonel C.W. Unthank, who had a mansion nearby.

Sussex Street was developed from about 1830 and has a mixture of terraces and cottages each with interesting period details.

The Crescent: In February 1821 a triangular piece of land was leased by John Bunn, a local builder, from the Joanna Scott Trust. A year later, No 1 of eighteen 'good and substantial' houses was ready, and The Crescent was completed by 1827. It remains surely one of the most elegant and unspoilt areas of Norwich – or any city!

The firm of Jarrold's, printers and stationers, has been in Norwich for over two centuries. Their main store overlooks the market and its London Street façade has a series of interesting terracotta panels, designed by Skipper in about 1900. Skipper had his office here for a time, and the panels reflect aspects of his own life.

In its heyday, the Royal Hotel was one of Norwich's most famous, and close enough to the station for convenience. It was designed by the local architect Edward Boardman and built 1896-7. In recent years it has been used by Anglia television.

Anyone could be fooled into thinking this building is an elegant church of the Wren period, but they would be wrong! It was built in 1924 as a bank, the local Headquarters of the then National Provincial Bank (later Nat. West). The architects were F.C.R. Palmer and W.F.C. Holden.

Ornate capitals spendidly painted on an old shop front in London Street, that of Mr Winsor Bishop. The firm of gold-smiths and silversmiths has been in existence since 1830. The street was called Cockney Lane in the eighteenth century from an old stream which ran from the 'Back of the Inns' into London Street and towards the market.

This building in Fye Bridge Street was once a pub called the 'Jack of Newbury'. The origin of the former pub's name goes back to the reign of Henry VIII, when John Winchcome, a wealthy clothier, supported his country by equipping 100 men to fight for the King. They did so at Flodden Field.

A man of great influence in the development of the Norwich parks and gardens was Arnold Sandys-Winsch (referred to as 'the Captain'), appointed as Superintendent of Parks in 1919. He was a gifted horticulturalist who had trained at Wisley (the H.Q. of the Royal Horticultural Society), and was articled to the celebrated landscape architect Thomas Mawson. In the period 1921-33 especially, he was responsible for the layout and design of Norwich's parks.

Eaton Park in Spring.

The yachting pond at Eaton Park.

Once every town had its gas works, but today few examples survive. Large gas-holders such as this one on Gas Hill, quite close to the river, stored gas ready for distribution, the inner 'roof' rising and falling. In the early days of gas there were no meters, so 'gas patrols' were necessary to check their customers' use!

Mousehold Heath is today a 190 acre expanse of heath and woodland, much loved by the citizens of Norwich – a slice of countryside on their doorsteps. Once it was much larger, and historically, is always linked with Kett's Rebellion. There are fine views over the city for those who wish to sit, or facilities for practising football for the more energetic.

Woods on Mousehold Heath in the early autumn.

The River Wensum is Norwich's ever-popular river, and the city's oldest highway. It was probably the 'Wendsome' originally, from its winding course. Along its banks grew the first Saxon settlement that was to become Norwich, and part of its route provided an effective defence, linked to the city walls.

'Pull's Ferry' (opposite) is the former watergate to the Cathedral. The Caen stone needed by the Norman builders passed from the river via a canal into the building areas of the Cathedral. The name today is taken from a former ferryman, John Pull, employed here 1796-1841. The house adjoining on the south side was for a time an inn, and Pull was the last to combine the jobs of ferryman and landlord!

Norwich's riverside is constantly evolving and new developments are starting to blend with the old. As with any river there is a fascination in the daily life on and around it, no more so than when it flows through the heart of a city. (Above) Towards the Millenium Bridge.

Looking in the opposite direction, towards the heart of the city.

Bishop Bridge is the only surviving medieval bridge to the city. It was built in the thirteenth century by the Bishop and Prior, and even had its own gatehouse. Queen Elizabeth I passed over it to visit the Earl of Surrey's palace at Mount Surrey.

Jarrold's Printing works: this impressive wedge-shaped red brick building, stretching upwards to five storeys, with a dome at one corner, was originally a yarn mill, but more recently part of the Jarrold's printing firm. The architect was the city surveyor, John Brown.

Reflections near Fye Bridge.

Norwich Art School from the river. This fine brick building was built by the city in 1899, first as a 'Technical Institute'. From 1901 it has been used as its Art School.

Shop windows at Christmas-time are somewhat special, as this example in White Lione Street shows.

126

Market-side trees appear to be growing electric bulbs as their wires merge with the branches.

Even much-loved views gain a touch of magic with a coating of snow.

Houses in the Close very quickly present Christmas card images.

Father Christmas's transport has improved a little these days!

'Ice Angel' was a fascinating addition to the 2004 Christmas scene in the city. It was commissioned by the City Council, with the Forum's participation, as part of the 'Spirit of Christmas' Festival. The sculptor was Jamie Hamilton who started with an 8 feet block of ice, and remarkably, used a chainsaw!

Mousehold Heath with the first covering of snow attracts children and adults.

*Skating is a popular participant and spectator sport and the new
facility outside The Forum is greatly enjoyed by both groups.*

Carrow Road is synonymous with football, and after a match, is a sea of green and yellow. Before its modern ground here, the Club played at another called 'The Nest' on the heights of Rosary Road. It is said that the mascot of a canary, leading to the club's nickname, originated with the pet birds favoured by the city's immigrant weavers.

The previous use of a building is there to see by looking up. This former bank building is in London Street, and is the work of George Skipper.

*Ornate barge-boards adorn this house in Magdalen Street, above our
normal eye level, so often missed.*

A bust from a Victorian house in Chapelfield North called St. Mary's Croft, a house with a fascinating history.

A coat of arms reflecting the fish-merchant's trade, is proudly displayed above a shop in Fye Bridge Street. The firm has been in the Howard family since it was started in 1889.

Congratulations to Magdalen Gates First School for an imaginative transformation of old school railings into a collection of brightly coloured pencils!

By a busy roundabout on St Crispin's Road is this Victorian toilet – a listed building no less, and a rare example of patterned concrete from this period. It is probably the oldest concrete urinal in the country.

140

There is a fascinating world of chimney pots in a city. It is strange how a chimney finishes off a house, as the modern trend towards adding 'artificial' chimneys bears out. This example is in The Crescent.

Street musicians of every kind often provide a 'lift' to busy shoppers. But a Scottish piper in full regalia is perhaps a little unusual.

The Sampson and Hercules: at the heart of this modern conversion, used as a dancehall for many years, lies a medieval manor house, built by Sir John Fastolf. This area of Tombland, apart from modern lettering and traffic, has changed little over the years.

Cricket under the shadow of a great cathedral –
a timeless image.